Isaac L. Ware

By the Pope's Command

Isaac L. Ware

By the Pope's Command

ISBN/EAN: 9783337042516

Printed in Europe, USA, Canada, Australia, Japan

Cover: Foto ©Lupo / pixelio.de

More available books at **www.hansebooks.com**

By the Pope's Command;

~ ~ OR ~ ~

THE DESTRUCTION OF THE BRITISH EMPIRE AND THE OVERTHROW OF PROTEST- ANTISM THROUGHOUT THE WORLD.

An Awful Glance at the Future

Price, $1.00.

PRESS OF
THE HUDSON-KIMBERLY PUBLISHING CO.
KANSAS CITY, MO.

PREFACE.

In writing this book, I want it distinctly understood that everything mentioned in it was revealed to me exactly as stated, and I can produce reliable witnesses to prove that on Monday, December 4, 1899, I related the whole dream or vision to them, word for word, just as it appears in this book. Up to that date, no remarks about the invasion of Canada or the midnight mass of the Roman Catholic Church had been heard or even thought of by me, as I take no interest in church or religious affairs, whatever; and furthermore, I know absolutely nothing about the percentatge of Roman Catholics in the Army and Navy of the United States or Great Britain, or their percentage of responsible positions in this or any other Protestant country. So far as I know, the dream or vision, or whatever it was, may have been the result of over-eating, or it may have been a true insight into the present state of existing affairs and a sure forecast of the future. Suffice it to say, we already hear threats of invading Canada and reorganizing the Clan-na-Gael, the Fenians, and other Catholic organizations.

BY THE POPE'S COMMAND;

OR,

The Destruction of the British Empire and the Overthrow of Protestantism throughout the World.

PART I.

CHAPTER I.

By some strange fatality, I was given an awful and startling view of the future, which I am at a loss to account for, as I am not religious or superstitious and am an unbeliever in fortune-telling or forecasts of any kind, which makes it all the stranger; however, I will now proceed to give an account of my strange experience, as far as I can remember. Just after eating a hearty meal on the afternoon of Sunday, December 3,

1899, I stretched myself out on the lounge at my home and began to read the different Sunday newspapers, which I had bought that morning. Soon I began to feel drowsy. A strange Maltese cat came in at the door, and sat down and looked at me fixedly for a few moments, and then he got up and walked slowly out. Now, if there is anything that is got up on crooked legs which I hate, it is a cat. Thought I, "Here is where I rid the world of a fine-looking cat," but I suddenly realized that I was utterly unable to move any part of my body. I wondered what on earth could be the matter with me. I tried to roll off the lounge, but it was no use. Then I began to think that I was dying, and the thought came to me that I was in a trance. What if my wife would suppose that I was dead, and have me buried? Then I renewed my efforts in trying to get up from there. "If I am really in a trance, what caused it?" I thought of that confounded cat—how he kept looking back at me as he went out. "Did he have anything to do with my present predicament?" I asked myself. No; it must have been something I had eaten for dinner that didn't agree with me. Then I began to think over the different things that I had eaten for dinner, when I suddenly realized that I was not alone, for I could hear someone moving about the room. Thought I, "It is the undertaker that has come to measure me for my coffin!" Then I strained every muscle in my body trying to get up, or, at least, trying to move one finger or toe, but my whole body seemed to be held in a vise. I could still hear heavy footsteps, but could not see anyone. 1 could hear the children playing and romping just outside of the window.

I discovered that I could move my eyes about, but not my head, so I began to look about to discover who my visitor was, and at the very first glance around I discovered him. He was a tall, dark-complexioned man of about forty-five or fifty years of age, with straight black hair, with a red fez cap on his head, and dressed like a Turk; he seemed to be busy arranging something in a large trunk-like box. I lay there watching him, unable to move a finger; I tried to move my head, then my feet, then my fingers and toes —all in vain. I felt that if I could just move one finger, I could then soon be able to get up. I tried again to roll off the lounge—all in vain. Then I resolved to remain calm and see what he was going to do. He fumbled around in the box awhile, and then he turned around and walked straight up to me, dragging a short, funny-looking, little red stool, the legs of which seemed to be set with diamonds and other precious stones that glittered and sparkled in a thousand different colors. He sat down on the stool and looked at me with his curious-looking eyes, that seemed to be coals of fire, and set deep in his head. He had a long, hook-like nose and high cheek-bones; the lower part of his face was covered with a heavy mustache and a long, thick, black beard.

I lay there wondering if my disbelief in the existence of the devil was about to be exploded, and just then he spoke for the first time. Said he:

"Knowing you to be non-sectarian, I have come to warn the whole world through you. Two terrible wars will soon be raging in this country; you will live to see the first one; and the terrible bubonic plague and the war combined will nearly depopulate this country. The war will be terrible—a religious war; no quarter will be asked or given, no prisoners will be taken. It will be a war between the allied powers of Europe, aided by the powerful Roman Catholic Church, on one side, and the Anglo-Saxons and all of the Protestant faith on the other. Blood will run through the streets of your cities like water, and then the world will see a strange thing occur; for the two races that are the most ostracized and discriminated against in the United States of America will take up arms and fight shoulder to shoulder with the Anglo-Saxon Protestants in defense of the American flag to the last ditch. The races referred to are the Jews and the

American Negroes. Nearly all the other races will oppose you in the field, with the possible exception of the Germans, for I cannot see the Germans as a nation opposing the Anglo-Saxon Protestants, but I can see a great many Germans opposing you. They are all members of the great Roman Catholic Church, the 'Church militant,' the disguised demon that has thrown out her long and powerful arms and grasped everything in this country that should belong to the Protestant alone—the Army, the Navy, the arsenals, the militia, the court-houses, the county offices, the city offices, the police departments, the fire departments, and the labor unions; who has special orders to strenuously oppose any attempt to increase the Regular Army above 25,000 men, hardly enough to keep order in one large city.

"Warn the President of the United States of America to be continuously on his guard, as his own life is in constant danger night and day, for the time for action is rapidly approaching, which will result in the end of

Protestant rule in Europe. It has even now commenced. Every regiment sent by England to South Africa has hundreds of Irish and other Catholics, with instructions to pick off all the Protestant officers, and the dispatches and cablegrams show how well they have done their work. A great Catholic nation in Europe is now preparing to make war on the Protestant British Government; they have already insulted the Queen; they are now awaiting some flimsy excuse to set the thousands upon thousands of their magnificent troops in motion; they have nothing to fear, for they know that in every British regiment there are hundreds of Catholic Irish soldiers, who, by killing off the British officers, will soon reduce the great British Army into a disorganized, panic-stricken mob. The United States of America will be called on for aid by the tottering British Government; then the Irish Catholics of North America will arm and openly invade Canada; they have nothing to fear; the Canadian Army, like the English Protestants, has already been fixed, and their officers will soon all be killed and their whole army routed and slain. No prisoners will be taken, and no quarter shown."

He then turned in his seat and made a motion towards the large box or trunk, and two more men, dressed exactly like him, came forward, carrying the box between them; reaching down in the box, they drew out a large map and raised it high above their heads and let go of it; the upper end kept going up until it touched the ceiling and stopped with a slight jolt; the lower end rested on the floor; then a bright light sprang up behind it, rendering it almost transparent. and such a wonderful map! It seemed to be alive. It was a map of the Old World— Europe, Asia, and Africa. He motioned for me to get up, and, to my astonishment, I discovered that I was able to rise without any extra effort on my part, where beforehand I was utterly unable to move. I stood on my feet.

"Come and see," said he.

I stepped forward to within three feet of the map. I saw all the different races of the Old World in their respective countries. I saw the large cities of Europe, Asia, and Africa. In every large city in Europe I saw large crowds of people gathered around the different newspaper offices, reading the bulletins. I looked down on the lower part of the map at South Africa; a battle had just begun between the Boers and English. I saw the puffs of smoke from thousands of small arms, and the flash, flash, flash of fire and heavy puffs of smoke from the hundreds of heavy cannon, that must have roared and echoed over the Transvaal hills for miles and miles. I saw what seemed at first a great moving cloud of dust, or whirlwind, but it proved to be a regiment of British cavalry; they came thundering around the side of a hill and charged with full speed upon a regiment of Boers; the British cavalry officers were riding in front of their troops with their swords raised high above their heads; the Boers opened fire, which emptied many a

British saddle; then the British cavalry began to fire right and left, wherever they saw an enemy.

My eyes seemed to follow the movements of three privates in the English cavalry. I saw them during the height of the battle raise their guns and take deliberate aim, not at the enemy, but at some of the Protestant officers of their own regiment. At the flash of their guns, three British line officers tumbled off their horses and lay stark and stiff on the ground. I saw the same thing repeated in different parts of the field. I saw that each of these assassins wore a small crucifix or small white pearl cross on his breast, suspended by a small chain around his neck; and one peculiar thing I noticed, was that, no matter in what position they were standing, the crucifix could be distinctly seen through their bodies, which seemed to be transparent, as far as seeing the crucifix was concerned. I noticed that their operations were not confined to the Protestant officers alone, for during the heat of battle I saw hundreds of private soldiers fall before their unerring aim.

While I still gazed at the map, I saw what was intended to be a midnight sortie of a British brigade on the Boer forts, or, rather, trenches. I saw the whole brigade drawn up in line, while the officers seemed to be giving instructions, for they would point with their swords in the direction of the enemy; finally, the order to advance seemed to be passed on down the lines, and the whole brigade began their march forward. I watched them with breathless interest. Nearer and nearer they approached the enemy's works; they were now crawling forward on hands and knees, and for the first time I noticed that this brigade were dressed in kilts or little short dresses. I began to look for the crucifix; there were few to be seen. Finally I selected one man who wore the crucifix, intending to keep my eye on him. Suddenly I saw the flash of a rifle in another part of the field; I looked quickly in that direction and saw the man who had fired the rifle. I saw his com-

rades angrily shaking their fists in his face.
I looked at him good; he did not wear the
small cross. Then suddenly the whole country was lit up by some kind of lights from the
Boers' forts or breastworks, and thousands
upon thousands of rifles and artillery were
turned loose on the betrayed British troops.
I looked for this rascal who had fired his
rifle; he was lying behind a great sheltering
rock, apparently unhurt. The whole regiment was now in a disorderly retreat down
the hill.

Was that rifle fired by accident or design?
Everything pointed to the latter theory; although this fellow was not a Catholic, his
sympathies seemed to be with the enemy.
"Well," thought I, "there are a good many
men in this world whose sympathies are
always with the enemies of their country.
We have them right here in the Congress of
the United States."

I understood at once why the British
Army fared so badly in every battle fought
in South Africa during the present war. I

also realized that if England expected to win in this or any other war, she must reorganize her army and navy; she must get rid of all of her rascally traitors in both army and navy.

I turned and asked him to show me the map of North and South America.

"Look," said he.

I turned once more to the map; it was now the map of North and South America. Naturally my eyes sought the city of Washington. Everything seemed to be in a panic. Newsboys were running through the streets with extra editions of the various newspapers. Crowds of people were in front of each newspaper office, reading the bulletins, and in some cases blocking up the whole street. I peered closely at the map. I could make out to read some of the bulletins, and read the following: "*Extra!* Canada invaded by Irish-Americans. The city of Windsor captured. Citizens fleeing for their lives. Rioting throughout the Dominion between Protestant and Catholic citizens. All business suspended. All moneys and securities are being hastily shipped to the United States. The Canadian army on the march to the relief of Windsor."

Just then I noticed an unusual commotion among the crowds of people in front of the bulletins; men stood on tiptoe and craned their necks to see the latest extra. I looked closely at the latest bulletin: *"Extra!!* A regiment of United States soldiers sent to patrol the Canadian-American border to prevent filibustering are attacked by American Roman Catholics. In the engagement that followed the American regiment lost 118 killed, 207 wounded; 9 officers were killed and 12 wounded. Loss of enemy not known, but supposed to be great. The high death-list in our regiment is supposed to be the work of foreign traitors on our own side. The whole country aroused. An extra session of Congress called to immediately reorganize the Army and Navy. The whole American Army now operating in the Philippines, Puerto Rico, and Cuba to be called home at once and reorganized. The President's message to Congress. The Philippines, Cuba, and Puerto Rico to be abandoned at once. All able-bodied male Negroes in the United States of America to be recruited, and, wherever it is necessary, drafted into the service of the Government."

As I stood gazing at the map, another bulletin extra went up. I read: *"Extra! ! !* France has declared war on the British Empire. All English and Americans ordered to leave France immediately. Catholic press and pulpit throughout the United States attack the Administration on account of American Army outrages on Catholic Church property in the Colonies. Secret meetings being held in all the Catholic Churches throughout the world. Arms and munitions of war being secretly shipped from Europe to Catholic priests in the United States of America. Catholics are openly drilling in defiance of American law. A crisis approaching. Panic in Wall Street. Runs on banks throughout the country. Money being withdrawn from banks and trust companies and hidden away in places of safety. Business at a standstill. Bread riots have begun. Stores, factories, and freight cars are being sacked and looted night and day. Throughout the country a reign of terror exists. Police refuse to protect life and property, and, to add to the already chaotic state of affairs, the bubonic plague has broken out and become epidemic in a large portion of the country, and, on account of the unsanitary conditions prevailing in all of the large cities, it is spreading rapidly, and will soon envelop the entire country. Rioting still continues. No authority of the law is recognized. Every man his own protector."

I stood there wondering what the next bulletin would be. I began to look over the map generally. I saw the American Army hurrying home from the Philippines, Puerto Rico, and Cuba. They were being landed in San Francisco, New York, and other cities on the east and west coasts of America, and as they marched through the streets, I noticed in all of the white regiments there were hundreds upon hundreds of men who wore the little white crucifix and seemed to have a fiendish, self-satisfied look on their faces. I turned my attention to the southern portion of the country. I saw what must have been over two million Blacks being drilled night and day by white Protestant officers. It seemed that days, weeks, and months passed while I stood there looking at that map, and it would fill a book of over 1,000 pages to relate the different scenes and incidents that I saw. It all seemed like a great moving panorama. I watched the tedious drilling of the blacks, and what seemed to me the slow reorganization of the Protestant army, for I now understood that both the American Army and Navy were to be Protestant absolutely.

"Why wasn't this done years ago," I asked of him who had first appeared to me, "and thus saved all of this bother?"

"Simply because some nations are over-trusting, and never recognize their real enemy until too late," he replied.

"How will this revolution end in this country, and what will be the outcome? Will this Government be overthrown like the British Empire, whose fall you have just predicted?"

"That," said he, "depends upon the time it will take to arm, drill, and equip their black troops, who will be used to guard property and keep order in the large cities until the white regiments are thoroughly reorganized. Any unnecessary delay in this matter will mean the complete overthrow of this nation."

"When will all of these troops be ready?" said I.

For answer he pointed to the map. There, from all parts of the United States, came the colored troops, thousands upon thousands—yes, hundreds of thousands upon hundreds of thousands. I scanned them closely, army after army, regiment after regiment. I was looking to see if any of them wore the cross or crucifix. I looked and searched in vain; there was no cross or crucifix among those fellows. I watched them as they would enter each large city, where, under the instructions of their white Protestant officers, everybody was driven off the streets, and martial law proclaimed. I saw them tacking up notices all over the cities that they entered, warning the people to keep off the streets. I looked again at the city of Washington. I saw the Capitol, Treasury buildings, and all the other Government buildings guarded by Negro troops. I looked at the cities of New York, Chicago, Cleveland, and St. Louis, and in all of these four cities I saw that th Negro troops had to fight their way through the streets, block after block. The religious fanatics would fire from windows and housetops on the colored soldiers as they passed in the streets below.

I began to look for the white soldiers; they had begun to reappear again, coming to reinforce the colored troops in the large cities. With the appearance of the white troops, and all of them Protestants, or supposed to be, confidence had been partly restored. The Roman Catholic agitators and known leaders were being given a short trial by the soldiers and shot to death. But the spirit of insurrection had not been entirely crushed out; rioting was still going on in the small cities and towns, and arson, pillage, and plundering were still going on wherever there were no soldiers stationed. In nearly every city and town of any consequence in this country the police, judges, and juries were nearly all Roman Catholics, and no mob except Protestant mobs were interfered with. All Protestants were either clubbed to death or shot by the police whenever they attempted to congregate anywhere.

I also saw the ravages of the bubonic or Asiatic plague, which was then epidemic. I saw the dead bodies of men, women, and children, all swollen up and turned black, lying in the streets and alleys. Hundreds were being buried or piled up on timbers and cremated by the soldiers, both white and black, who were dying by the hundreds themselves. The reorganization of the Army and Navy was still going on, although it was not as thorough as it should have been, for there were still hundreds of men among the white troops wearing the little white crucifix of Rome.

"Well," thought I, as I stood before the map and saw the condition of affairs, "this will forever settle the race problem in th's country, but it will give birth to another problem a thousand times worse than the race problem could ever attain. It will be the religious problem now, and will compel the United States to become a military Government. Large bodies of soldiers will have to be stationed close to all of the large cities in this country, for the United States of America will then be just like the different Governments of Europe: freedom of speech will be done away with, and every man that criticises the Government will do so at his peril, and our prominent Roman Catholic representatives and senators will no longer be permitted to stand up in the Congress of the United States and dictate the policy of this Government."

At least, that is the way I thought it out as I looked at the map, which suddenly began to roll up, after which it dropped lightly to the floor and another one was hastily brought forward. As it unrolled, I saw it was the map of the Old World, and that the whole of Europe and Asia and a great part of Africa was in an active state of warfare. It was bewildering at the first glance, but I began to realize how matters stood, or, rather, moved, for everything that could move was moving; armies were on the march; battles were being fought; war-ships of all the great nations of Europe and Asia were on the seas, some headed one way, some another; transports were loading and unloading troops in the different parts of Europe and Asia.

The longer I studied the map the better I understood the situation: France and

England were at war; Russia and Germany had attacked China and Japan; the Turks and all the Mohammedans, including all of British India, were fighting Germany, Austro-Hungary, and Russia. I saw the millions of Mohammedan soldiers with their red fez caps and picturesque uniforms of short, baggy pants and Zouave jackets. I saw the soldiers of China, Persia, Afghanistan, Arabia, British India, Turkey, and Japan, all facing the Russian Army, whose lines extended along almost the entire southern boundary line of Russia. But, in spite of their great army, the Russians were outnumbered over five to one, for all of the dark races of the Old World had turned out their full strength, for they seemed to understand that it was to be a war of extermination. On all sides were to be seen war and pestilence, for the bubonic plague had now enveloped the whole world; men seemed to prefer death by the bullet or sword rather than face the terrible scourge.

I turned once more to my strange entertainer, and asked him what the outcome in Europe was to be.

Said he: "The nations of Europe and Asia will suffer the same fate as the Mound-builders and Cliff-dwellers of old, who wer· exterminated by war and pestilence. It is the work of Nature. Everything that lives must die, even great nations. This world has stood for countless millions of years; it has been populated and depopulated thousands upon thousands of times; war and pestilence have exterminated much greater and more powerful nations than exist on this earth to-day. Nature is never at rest; she creates, exterminates, and regenerates with a precision that is omnipotent, awful, and irresistible."

Pointing at the map on which the different nations of Europe and Asia were drawn up in battle array, he continued: "There is absolutely nothing short of total extinction of one or both factions that will ever bring peace, for the different nations that you see opposing each other have utterly lost all confidence in each other, and this war will continue to the bitter end, and those who escape the gun and sword will soon fall victims of the plague, until not one will be left to tell the tale. It is only a repetition of Nature's awful laws; it is only the inevitable.

As I still looked at the map I saw great earthquakes that sent tidal waves mountains high around the earth. It seemed to me that the very elements had taken hold in order to hurry matters along.

While still noting the effect of the earthquakes, the map rolled up and dropped to the floor, and another one was run up. It was the map of North and South America; or, rather, the Western Hemisphere. Naturally my eyes rested on the United States and Canada. What a change had been wrought all over the whole Dominion of Canada! I could see the French flag waving over all the forts and public buildings—but not alone, though, for I could also see that the green banner of Erin was quite numerous, thus explaining the disastrous results to the Canadian Protestants far better than words could do. It showed the work of the Pope and priests of Rome, who have long looked on the whole of North America with longing eyes. I looked at the United States of America: War and pestilence were still the order of the day. Urged on by the Pope of Rome, France, Italy, and Austria had attacked the United States.

Said my strange visitor: "The midnight masses held in all of the Catholic churches were held in order to formulate a plan of attack. Your Romanist citizens, who practically control the Army and Navy and politics in this country, are to give the Papal armies of France, Italy, and Austria all the assistance possible, and they are compelled to do it—it is the Pope's command, and must be obeyed, and will be obeyed to the letter."

I began to look the map over: the rioting and plundering as shown to me in the first map of North America was still going on; I saw great powder mills blown up in different parts of the country; the greater portion of the Army was being hurried to the Pacific, Atlantic, and southern coasts of the country to repel the invaders of Europe, leaving only a small portion to guard the inland cities; all of the heavy ordnance of Sandy Hook forts, Wadsworth, Hamilton, and Governor's Island had been permanently disabled, rendering them practically useless; in fact, there was scarcely a single piece of ordnance, light or heavy, along the whole coast of the country, that was not disabled or destroyed. By whom? The Army and Navy officials had been unable to determine.

Noticing that my curious-looking entertainer was preparing to take his leave, I spoke. Said I: "You have shown me the destiny of the different nations of the earth, and you claim that you came to warn them through me. Now, what shall I tell the people of North America, and what shall I say to those of the Eastern Hemisphere?"

Said he: "Tell the Protestant people of North America that war and pestilence are inevitable and *sure*. Tell them to prepare for it at once by getting rid of all Romanists in their Army and Navy and political offices. Your labor unions are practically controlled by them. A priest can put a stop to rioting quicker than the President of the United States could. They don't even respect the neutrality laws of this country. They are the slickest bribers and political schemers this world ever produced. Their hatred and contempt of the Protestants are so intense that they will openly attack you in the streets. If you attempt to expose them, you will find a great many Protestant orators who will get up and champion the Romanists' cause; turn these Protestant orators out with them. No delay must be tolerated; the present is a situation that calls for prompt and radical action. Organize your Protestant societies. Drill and equip your able-bodied male Negroes; they can be trusted. The Pope certainly knew what he was talking about when he said, 'We can have this country in ten years. There are two points to consider, the American Indian and the Negro.' He well knew that he already has enough Romanists in the American Army and Navy to prevent them from doing any effectual work, and if they could Romanize the Negro, they could present a solid front to the Protestant Americans. Every one of their soldiers would be recruited by the priests of their respective parishes, thus preventing any Protestant from getting in their ranks, for the priests personally know every Roman Catholic, man, woman, or child, in their parishes, and the Protestant would get no chance to get into their ranks to play the traitor; while, on the other hand, the Protestants would have to take any man who they thought was all right, and in the very first battle they would lose every one of their officers, and their whole army would be routed and slain. But the Pope has found out that he *cannot Romanize the Negro.* That is one reason why the blow has not been struck. He knows that the white Protestants can recruit about two million Negro troops, who will tumble over each other to enlist, the moment they realize that the country is actually in danger. This Negro race has never produced a traitor to the American flag, and absolute reliance can be placed in them to hold the foreign Romanists in check until the Protestant Americans can reorganize their Army and Navy.

"That," said he, "is the secret of the Irish hatred of the American Negro; he is a standing menace to them, and is a hard customer to meet on the battle-field, and will always be a confirmed Protestant. So the Pope has abandoned the idea of Romanizing the American Negro, and is now plotting with the French Government, who, with the aid of the Irish Romanists, will certainly overthrow the British Empire, as foretold on the maps that I have just shown to you. Then Canada will fall, and the United States will be attacked by the allied armies of France, Italy, and Austria and thousands of Roman Catholics from South America, which is growing more hostile towards this country every day. The Romanists in this country will give you no end of trouble, and will harass and handicap the Protestant Americans on every side, causing an almost complete suspension of business of every kind.

"And last, but not least," said he, "tell the American Protestants to stop their senseless prejudice and ostracism toward the black people of this country. There is no just cause for it, and it should be discontinued at once."

"Now, what shall I say to the English people?" said I, as I glanced at the map just in time to see the French and Italian warships begin shelling New York City and Brooklyn.

Said he: "Tell them to withdraw their troops from the Transvaal while they have some officers left. Order them back to England, and prepare for the great and final struggle. Nothing but disaster and death awaits them in the Transvaal. The Turkish or Japanese Army could have routed and driven the Boers into the sea long ago."

"And why?" I exclaimed.

"Because," said he, "there are no traitors in the armies of either one of those two nations; every man is loyal to his ruler and country. And when the same conditions prevail in the Army and Navy of the United States of America, then, and not until then, will the Americans be invincible in war and formidable to all evilly disposed nations or races of the earth."

My strange visitor grabbed his diamond-beset stool and hurried out of the door, and his two assistants followed, carrying the large box between them. I turned to look at the map. It was gone. My wife was standing near the door, looking curiously at me.

"What on earth is the matter with you?" she exclaimed. "You have been standing there looking at the wall and asking questions about nearly every nation on the face of the globe. Are you feeling sick?"

"No," said I; "I only had a dream, or a trance, I don't know which."

I looked down at the carpet, and the imprint of the legs of that little, red, diamond-bedecked stool could still be faintly seen.

CHAPTER II.

That night my mysterious visitor reappeared, this time alone.

Said he: "There is great rejoicing in Ireland. The long-looked-for opportunity has arrived. It has long been the prayer of the Roman Catholic Church that the haughty and arrogant British Protestant nation would become involved in war with some other power, and thus enable the down-trodden Irish race to strike their long-delayed and decisive blow for liberty and self-government. The time has arrived; the blow is being struck, and will continue to be struck until the final overthrow of the hated British nation, and the ghost of Protestantism is forever driven from the green soil of Ireland. The good St. Anthony has decreed it, and the epitaph of the great and good Robert Emmet will soon be written."

Said I: "Your sympathy seems to have changed since you were here last."

"I have no sympathy for either side," said he. "I am only stating the facts. Did you pay strict attention to the maps? Did you note the real cause of British disasters? Did you see the stampede of the ammunition mule-train, and the cause? Did you see the surrender of the Royal Irish Fusileers?"

"I saw it all very plainly and understood," I answered.

"Then," said he, "go and warn the whole world, as I have commanded, for the British nation is even now struggling on the ragged edge of total destruction, and the war will extend to her North American possessions. War and insurrection will extend, and soon envelop the whole of North America, including Mexico and a greater part of South America. It is inevitable and *sure*."

"Is it too late for the British Empire to avert the coming disaster?" I asked.

"Well, not entirely," he answered.

"Then what would you suggest?" I inquired.

Said he: "I never suggest; I simply explain the sure and only remedy for existing evils, and that remedy is to immediately discontinue their operations with her white troops. Arm and equip all of her black subjects from the West Indies, Australia, and New Zealand, and Africa, and her brown and yellow subjects of East India. Let them form the privates; place them under white Protestant officers, with never a white man in the ranks as private; make it impossible for a single white soldier to get into the ranks. Then the world would find out that the Boers are not such sharpshooters as was generally supposed, for the British losses of both officers and men would immediately fall off at least 70 per cent; for, being unable to get into the ranks of the dark-skinned soldiers without detection, the papal assassins' occupation would be gone. The whole war in South Africa can be fought and won with the same set of officers that takes charge of the campaign, and the British nation still has this one chance to snatch victory from otherwise sure defeat."

"But," said I, "suppose they pay no attention to this advice."

"In that case," said he, "nothing but sure defeat and annihilation awaits them. And," continued he, "they should learn wisdom from experience. Their recent heavy loss of officers is without record and unprecedented, and in the annals of warfare since time immemorial it stands without a single parallel."

CHAPTER III.

"Before I leave you," said he, "you must see the future map of the world."

He handed me a small map of the world, and I at once began to look at North and South America. Cuba and all of the islands of the West Indies had disappeared, and, in their places, there were four large volcano mountains, all within a few hundred miles of each other; and from the Gulf of Campeachy to the Bay of Panama the land had all disappeared, and it was now all open sea. Volcanoes were active all over Old Mexico, or, rather, what was left of Old Mexico, for there was very little left of it. Lower California had disappeared entirely, and, in fact, nearly all of California had sunk out of sight, and the Sierra Nevada Mountains were now the coast line; Nevada and Arizona were filled with great bodies of water, some of them larger than Lake Superior; there were also several active volcanoes in both of these States, or Territories, whichever they are; the lower part of Florida had disappeared; New Orleans was no longer on the map; two of the Great Lakes were dry—I think Lake Superior and Lake Huron—and the other lakes were nearly dry; Chicago seemed to be at least five miles from the waters of Lake Michigan; great clouds of steam-like vapor arose out of the beds of the empty lakes; Niagara River had long been dry, and the great rocks where the falls used to be were grown all over with vegetation.

I noticed a strange-looking flag over a large fort or barracks, where some soldiers were stationed. It was different from any I had ever seen. It had a crown and a large double cross, like this $-\!\!+\!\!-$ and three stripes —I think they were red, purple, and green. The soldiers' uniforms were dark green.

"Where are the Stars and Stripes of the United States of America?" I asked, "and where are the Anglo-Saxon Protestants?"

"There are no more Anglo-Saxon Protestants," was the answer; "they were overthrown nearly nine hundred years ago. Their flag is now only kept as a relic. There is only one religious denomination now in this country, and that is Catholic. This is no longer a republic; the rulers are chosen by the Pope, and whose power is absolute."

"And the Protestants were overthrown at last, were they?"

"Yes," he exclaimed. "There were two wars, the first was long and bloody, and the Anglo-Saxons succeeded in beating their enemies off and held the country two hundred and sixty years, but were overthrown, exterminated, or driven out of the country. But," said he, "this second war will not occur during your lifetime or the lifetime of your children. Your great-great-grandchildren will live to see it, and be killed in it. It will be a terrible conflict, and ·will last over six years, for the Anglo-Saxons and their Negro allies will fight until they are nearly totally exterminated."

—44—

He took the map out of my hand, waved me a good-night, and was gone. I heard a piercing scream, and leaped out of bed; my little two-year-old boy was sitting up in his bed, looking fearfully out of the door, which was standing wide open. I closed the door, and asked him what was the matter. He only clung to me and pointed at the door. I put him in the bed with his mamma.

"What is the matter with the baby?" my wife asked.

"I do not know," I replied.

"Open the damper in the stove," she continued; "the room is full of gas."

"There is no fire in that stove," said I; "the stuff that you smell is sulphur—yes, madam, the Simon-pure sulphur, and I guess I will sit up the balance of the night." Which I did.

CHAPTER IV.

Now, if this vision proves to be a true forecast of the future, then the course in the future is plain, as there are only two great Protestant nations in existence on earth to-day. They must either stand together or fall separately. Let England be overthrown, and the United States will soon have to fight the whole of Catholic Europe and South America, and probably Mexico thrown in. To array the Anglo-Saxons against each other is a well-laid Roman Catholic trap, and a whole lot of consummate idiots in the Congress of the United States have already fallen into it.

CHAPTER V.

The Horrors of the Bubonic or Asiatic Plague.

In studying those maps as seen in my vision, I took more notice of the progress of the bubonic plague than any other thing, and if it is coming true, the nations of the earth had better be preparing to *fight it* instead of *fighting each other;* for this strange being that I saw in my vision said it is positively coming, and will spread all over the earth, and it and the wars combined will totally depopulate a large portion of this earth. As some of the things that I saw on those maps have already happened since then, I have no reason to doubt that the whole thing will happen just as it was forecast, although I hardly believed that the Catholics would give the country any real trouble soon, but it is best to be prepared. A thief won't attempt to rob you if he knows that you are "on to him" and prepared for him; he will want to take you unawares.

But to return to my subject: I saw people dying like poisoned flies all over this country. Nearly all the large cities were almost totally deserted, the people having fled to the country to avoid the plague. All the cities were garrisoned by soldiers, white and colored, who were themselves falling victims to the terrible scourge. A man's life didn't seem much to these soldiers, for hardly was a person's body cold before he was thrown on a pile with many others, great buckets full of oil were thrown on them, lighted torches were applied, and, as the flames roared and crackled around them, the soldiers leaned on their rifles and looked on with a hard, stony stare, and more bodies were unloaded and tossed on the burning pile without any ceremony whatever.

As I looked at the hard, set faces of those soldiers, I wondered what on earth had become of human nature; but I reasoned that death had lost all its terrors for them, and it was to them now only a matter of business, and they were resigned to their own fate, which it seemed was inevitable and near. It seemed that the people who fled to the country districts to avoid the plague were faring no better than those left in the cities, for they, too, were dying by the hundreds. There seemed to be no escape.

Now, as all my dreams invariably come true, I certainly believe this vision is worth consideration, and the best thing this Government can do is to immediately call all her soldiers and citizens home from all the foreign countries, wherever they may be, and then close all our seaports to immigration and international commerce of every sort whatsoever, and keep them closed until the plague in foreign countries has run its course or has been stamped out entirely.

PART II.

THE RACE PROBLEM.

There exists in this country to-day what is called "the vexed race problem." Various remedies have been suggested for the betterment of the same by a number of our greatest and most distinguished orators and statesmen. Some have suggested the deportation of the Negro race to some other continent, while some have even suggested intermarriage, by which the black race would be finally absorbed, but the fallacy of the latter is too evident to be discussed here. Various other remedies have been introduced to show how it could be settled, but we still have the race problem, and will continue to have it until Nature finally steps in and settles it; for it is one of Nature's inexplicable laws and can and will be attended to at the proper time, and settled for all time to come, by Nature alone. The process has already commenced. Nature seems to work in a roundabout way, but a careful study of it will show that she works straight and to the point.

Yes, the process of settling the race problem in this country is already well under way. We have in this country a sect that holds the laws of their church (whose head is in a foreign country) above the laws of this Government, and that considers their children too good to attend our public schools, and tries to besmirch and belittle the characters of some of our best army officers, who risked their lives for the American flag in the Philippines. They have tried for years to plunge this country into a war with Great Britain, but it has been and always will be a signal failure; for the great Anglo-Saxon race, that is capable of building up and governing a great country like this, is capable of keeping its "weather eye" on a sect that disrespects its laws and holds church above state. And when the invasion of Canada is attempted, it will be the signal for a general all-around war between the two religions, or, rather, the Roman Catholics of the world against the Anglo-Saxon Protestants—and of course the Negro will side with the American Protestants. And when the Americans realize that of all the different races of man in this country the American Negroes are the only ones that are loyal to a man, then all race prejudice will immediately disappear, and the Negro will stand forth recognized as an American citizen and a man. All discrimination against him in trade, business, or industrial pursuits will be removed. The white Protestants of this country will show their appreciation of the black men, for their steadfast loyalty to the American flag, by placing them in good positions of trust and by educating those that are not educated, and opening the doors of all industrial pursuits to them, thus placing them on a level with any other race in this country; while the Negro will show his devotion to the Protestant American by living up to the laws of the land and conducting himself in an honest, honorable, and law-abiding manner. And thus Nature will solve the vexed race problem, without any deportation of the Negro or intermarriage.

I may be mistaken, but I believe everything that I saw in my vision will come to pass just as predicted. Look at the infamous attempts to besmirch the characters of the Twentieth Kansas Regiment and its officers. Just trace up the different tirades of abuse hurled at this famous regiment and its officers, and see who the accusers and abusers are. Look at the open violation of our neutrality laws every day since the war in the Transvaal began. Take any Romanist newspaper and read their opinion of the President of the United States; yes, read their own newspapers, printed and edited by them, and see what you think about it. All of these things I regard as the work of Nature, which will eventually end in the solving of the race problem in this country.

The Anglo-Saxon Protestant is a quiet, indulgent, and forbearing race, in peace; but once thoroughly stirred up and a more terrible, uncompromising, and fighting race does not exist on this earth to-day. Any attempt by any of the alien races in this country to override the laws of this country will only result in disaster to the law-breakers, and will certainly solve the race problem, as far as the black man is concerned; for the Negro will never take up arms against the dear old Stars and Stripes, or attempt to besmirch or belittle the brave men who have followed it to victory or death, for stamped in the heart of every American Negro are the sentiments: "Here's to the American flag, always in the right; but, right or wrong, here's to the flag!" Such steadfast devotion must and will bring its reward, sooner or later. The Negro doesn't consider it his business to inquire who is right or who is wrong when the flag is attacked, but takes up arms and defends the old flag to the direst extremity, and leaves the question of right or wrong to be argued out afterwards.

It is not patriotism that prompts the Negro to be loyal to the American flag; for, if he ever had any patriotism, it has long been crushed out by the many abuses and indignities that have been heaped upon him in this country. Every race is put ahead of the Negro; even the blanketed Indian, whom it is almost impossible to civilize, is considered better than the Negro. Now, can anyone wonder at the Negro's lack of patriotism? He has nothing to be patriotic about. The explanation of the Negro's loyalty to the American flag is this: it is the flag of his country, the land of his birth. He knows no other country, he knows no other flag; and when war breaks out, he will take up arms with the same unconcern that he now takes up his dinner-bucket, and will follow the flag and defend it with his life, if necessary. And why? His country has been attacked, and this is the flag of his country; he must defend his country, he must defend its flag. And when the bugle sounds the charge, his heart quickens, but not with patriotism—he has long since lost all of that. He has but few thoughts, and they are to charge right in on the enemy, kill them right and left, and drive them out of their works. So, with a yell of defiance and derision, they sweep on to the charge like thousands of demons let loose from hell.

I once heard an old army officer say that the terrible yells of defiance that only the black regiments are capable of giving are enough to strike terror to the hearts of the bravest, and, once heard, are never to be forgotten. It is not the loud, ringing chee· of patriotism that is given by the white regiments, but a loud, terrible yell of defianc· and derision. It is the same menacing yell that the white man has heard all throug!i the dark continent of Africa, wherever the black man was engaged in battle. It was heard on San Juan Hill and at El Caney, in Cuba, when the black American troops charged, and drove the Spaniards out of their block-houses and trenches, and saved the Rough Riders from total extermination.

What will the great civilized nations of the earth think when they come to know that the United States of America has nearly nine millions of these loyal subjects, who have lost every ounce of patriotism on account of indignities and abuse that have been heaped upon them for years? And can it be wondered at that patriotism has long been dead in their hearts? They are discriminated against on every side. Let some Negro who imagines that he is patriotic take a ride through the South in the "Jim Crow" cars, and it will knock the patriotism out of him in a hurry. This is only one of the many thousands of cases I could cite, but they are too well known to discuss here. And in the face of all this injustice the Negroes remain loyal—not patriotic, but loyal.

But better times are coming for this down-trodden race. Nature has taken hold, and the dawn of a brighter day will soon be breaking. "It is a long lane that has no turning." But Nature has traveled nearly the whole length, and is fast approaching the turning-point, and the race problem will be settled before this Government is finally overthrown.

CONCLUSION.

The United States Government ought to send all of these Boer and Filipino sympathizers out of this country, without regard to race, religion, social or political standing; send them to the countries that they sympathize with; send them as fast as they can be rounded up and loaded on cattle-ships. Begin with Pettigrew, Tillman, Atkinson, Mason, and a host of others that this country can spare. We will have that many the less to contend with when war breaks out in this country. Of course they won't fight themselves, but, like the cavalry bugler, they are liable to sound the charge in which thousands of men may lose their lives. So the Government cannot get rid of them any too soon, as nothing but loyal citizens are needed or wanted. This country is at war with a foreign race now, and they are enough to contend with at present, and there is no room here for traitors, agitators, or conspirators.

Before I close this book, I wish to ask a few pertinent questions of the different agitators and fault-finders in this country. In the first place, we will suppose the civilized world to be one large school, and all the different nations of the earth the pupils. The two Anglo-Saxon nations are the bullies of the school, or, rather, they have never been whipped in a fight with any of the other pupils; consequently they are hated and feared by all the other pupils, who, knowing them to be related by blood, dare not attack one for fear of having to fight them both. Now it is a well-known fact that should the bully of the school get into a fight with a small but tough little boy, and fail to give him a sound thrashing, then the bully at once becomes the laughing-stock of the whole school; they don't even respect him, much less fear him, and the bully at once becomes a "back number" and a "has been"; the smaller boy in school will make faces at him, and the bully must stand it, for all fear of him has vanished; and if he strikes even the smallest boy now, they will pile on him and "knock thunder" out of him. These are the exact conditions that confront the great Anglo-Saxon nations to-day. They must conquer the Boers and Filipinos or become the laughing-stock of the world.

How would Mr. Pettigrew and the rest of his advocates like to see their country a laughing-stock for the rest of the world, and barred out of some and discriminated against in every commercial sea-port in the world, and utterly unable to enforce a single demand, for fear of a combined attack of all the European powers? Talk about your large standing armies! This Government would have to keep an army of at least 3,000,000 men continually under arms, and a navy of such magnitude as to be a continual menace to consolidated Europe, as we would have to be prepared to back up every demand we made on allied Europe with a force superior to any they could raise; for, once we lose our prestige, nothing but force will go.

Has Mr. Pettigrew lost all his patriotism and foresight, or is he going crazy?

The End.

NOTE.—This book has been withheld from publication for certain reasons; but, with the appearance of a certain female agitator in this country, whose sole purpose is to stir up trouble, and in open defiance of our neutrality laws, I considered it about time to sound the warning. We have enough agitators of our own, without importing any foreign ones. What we want in this country is peace and tranquillity—not war and strife. The Government should give the lady her passports at once, by all means.